Why Puppies
Do That

Why Puppies Do That

A Collection of Curious Puppy Behaviors

Tom Davis

Illustrations by Katherine Zecca

WILLOW CREEK PRESS

Published by Willow Creek Press, P.O. Box 147, Minocqua, Wisconsin 54548

Editor: Andrea K. Donner

Library of Congress Cataloging-in-Publication Data

Davis, Tom, 1956-
    Why puppies do that : a collection of curious puppy
behaviors / Tom Davis ; illustrations by Katherine Zecca.
        p.cm.
    ISBN 978-1-59543-592-7 (hardcover : alk. paper)
    1. Puppies–Behavior–Miscellanea. I. Title.
    SF433.D39 2007
    636.7'07–dc22

                                        2007011292

Printed in the United States

Contents

Introduction

When my stepdaughter, Sophia, was eight years old—about the time she became my stepdaughter, in fact—my English setter, Emmylou, had a litter of puppies. We set up a whelping box in the basement, suspended a heat lamp over it for warmth, and watched in delight and astonishment as, over the course of several hours, Emmy brought seven new lives into the world. Tiny and helpless, with squashed-up, blunt-nosed faces, ears the size of quarters, stumpy legs, and tails like pencil stubs, there was a distinct sense of the unformed about them, as if they were lumps of clay that a sculptor had made a start on and then set aside to come back to later.

Truth to tell, we witnessed few if any actual births. The ancient protective instincts kick in, and like the wolf mothers from which all dogs are descended Emmy preferred to deliver her pups when no eyes but hers were there to see it. We'd leave the room for a few minutes, and upon our return she'd be licking another puppy into shape, rolling the wet, lumpy cylinder of its body from one side of the box to the other. Emmy wasn't necessarily the gentlest mama, but she ran a tight ship.

We watched the puppies grow and change—a process that happens so fast at that age you'd swear you can see a difference not just from one day to the next, but between breakfast and lunch. After their eyes opened and they started to get their legs under them we'd tuck a blanket into a wicker laundry basket, place the pups in it, and take them outside, where we'd turn them loose in the back yard to explore. Emmy would come along, too, thankful for the opportunity to stretch her legs but always keeping a watchful eye on her brood. The pups were tentative at first, unsure of themselves and of the dazzling sights, sounds, and, in particular, smells that seemed to come at them from every direction, but it didn't take long for them to get past their trepidation. Soon they were drinking it all in, romping around, sniffing everything, eager to satisfy their curiosity about this big new world. Their ears flopped, their legs and tails went every which way, their irresistible puppy faces wore expressions of sheer exuberance, of unbridled, unaffected joy.

When the pups were well on their way to being weaned and spending more and more time outdoors, my wife's elderly uncle stopped by one afternoon. A gruff, flinty sort—an old curmudgeon if there ever was one—we led him to a chair in the sun and opened the gate to the puppy pen. Uncle Jim never knew what hit him. In the blink of an eye, he was being swarmed by puppies. They were literally crawling on top of each other trying to get into his lap—and the smile he wore could have lit up the dark side of the moon. It was a side of him that we knew existed, but that we glimpsed very, very rarely. And we had the puppies to thank for it.

Sophia had a part in all of this, helping me with the pups, handling them on a daily basis, playing with them and proudly showing them off to her friends—who, in turn, handled and played with and generally fussed over the puppies themselves. You hear a lot about the importance of puppies being given proper "socialization"—it's been harped on so relentlessly that it's become a mantra among dog people—but no one who raises a litter of pups in proximity to kids has anything to worry about. By the time the pups are ready to go to their new homes, they'll have gotten all the stimulation they need, and then some, to ensure that the psychological machinery is humming along at peak efficiency, and they'll have nothing but positive feelings about the human race.

Inevitably, the time did come for Emmy's puppies to leave. We were sad to see them go, of course, but I assured Sophia that their new owners would love them and take just as good care of them as she had, and that because she'd done such a great job helping to raise them they'd have no trouble adjusting to their new surroundings. Sophia has always had a pragmatic streak, and this seemed to make sense to her.

When she went back to school that fall—she must have been in the third grade then—one of her first assignments was to write a report on the topic "How I Spent My Summer." Among other recollections, Sophia wrote the following: *Our dog had puppies. It was the neatest thing I have ever seen.*

I can tell you about how much it cost to produce that litter of puppies, and exactly what the people who bought pups paid for them. But I don't know how you put a price on what they meant to a certain eight-year-old girl.

Tom Davis
Green Bay, Wisconsin

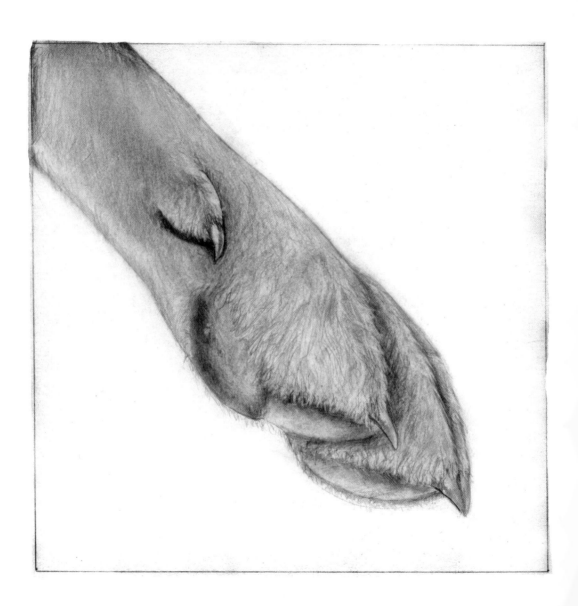

Why do puppies have dewclaws?

Down in the swamps and canebrakes, there are backwoodsmen who swear on Stonewall Jackson's grave that a dog born with dewclaws on its hind legs is "natch'ral snakeproof"—immune to the effects of a venomous snakebite, that is. And they'll back up this claim by trotting out a rawboned hound, showing you the curved, thumb-like claws on the inside of its hind legs, and telling you that the dog's been snakebit more than once but that the dewclaws "sucked up the poison."

Essentially a fifth toe that occupies a position on the canine foot analogous to the human thumb, the dewclaw is a remnant from a time in the distant past—as in over 40 million years ago—when the dog's ancestors climbed trees. Having five toes was an advantage then, but as these proto-canids evolved into a ground-dwelling species that relies on its speed and agility afoot to capture prey, the fifth toe became redundant and, over time, receded to become the vestigial digit it is today. It's not uncommon for the dewclaw to be completely absent from the hind legs of many breeds, although there are a few—notably the Great Pyrenees and the Briard—that have a *double* set of hind dewclaws. Claims of snakeproofing aside, the question of whether dewclaws serve any useful purpose, whether they pose a potential hazard (inadvertently scratching a cornea, for example, or catching and tearing on obstructions), and whether they should be removed shortly after whelping (when it's a simple and relatively painless procedure) continue to be hotly debated by dog folk.

How can puppies from the same litter have different sires?

This sort of gives new meaning to the phrase "Who's your daddy?" All kidding aside, this is for real. It can happen, and it does—although ethical, conscientious breeders try very hard to see that it doesn't. The technical term for this phenomenon, by the way, is "superfecundation."

There are a variety of factors that allow it to occur, the most obvious being that female dogs produce multiple ova (eggs). This is the reason dogs have litters of puppies rather than individual ones. Yeah, I know, *duh*. But it's somewhat more complicated than that. When dogs ovulate, the ova, or oocytes, are still immature. They don't become fully mature until two and one-half to three days following ovulation (although they're capable of being penetrated by sperm during this period), and they remain viable for two to seven days after that. Canine sperm can remain viable in the reproductive tract for up to eight days… So you do the math. The bottom line is that because (A) dogs are polygamous breeders, and (B) females remain receptive to males for a week or more, the sperm of multiple sires can potentially find itself in position to uphold the family honor.

So who *is* your daddy?

Why are puppies born with their eyes closed?

All mammals have evolved complex "strategies" for reproduction, gestation, and development that, given the environmental conditions that have shaped them and the ecological niche they occupy, optimize their chances for survival and perpetuation of the species. In the whitetailed deer, for example, the gestation period is fairly long—about six and one-half months—but the fawns are very precocious, able to stand, walk, see, hear, and respond to danger within minutes of birth.

The various canines have taken a somewhat different tack. The gestation period in dogs is only about two months—58 to 63 days, on average—the trade-off being that the puppies are not nearly as far along as the young of some other species. Newborn puppies are, in fact, helpless; you could almost say that while not technically premature, they're in a sense neo-natal. The basic reason that puppies are born with their eyelids tightly shut, then, is that the eye itself is still developing. It's extremely fragile, needing all the protection it can get not only from from foreign objects (grit, dirt, etc.) and potential pathogens but from bright light that could damage the eye's delicate photoreceptors and optic mechanisms. Even so, an occasional pup contracts an eye infection *in utero* from its mother, and because it's so difficult (if not impossible) to detect any symptoms with the eyes clamped shut, loss of vision, and loss of the eye itself, are real possibilities.

Most puppies begin to open their eyes at about two weeks of age, although several more weeks must elapse before their eyes—and their eyesight—are fully developed.

Why are puppies' eyes always blue when they first open them?

Again, it comes back to the fact that at the time they begin to open, usually at about two weeks of age, the puppy's eyes are still immature. In this instance, the pigment in the iris—the "colored" portion of the eye—remains undeveloped. And in much the same way that the shorter wavelengths of sunlight are "scattered" by molecules in the atmosphere to produce the appearance of blue sky—"Rayleigh scattering," this is called, after the English physicist who first described it in the 1870s—light entering the lightly pigmented iris scatters, reflects, and appears to *our* eyes as some shade of blue. A milky, grayish-blue is typical, but some puppy's eyes appear ice blue, while others are almost green. As the pigment "fills in" over the following weeks and months, the eyes of most puppies grow darker, ultimately becoming whatever hue, from pale yellow gold to nearly black, the palette of genetic inheritance has painted for them. The exceptions are those breeds, such as Siberian huskies and Australian shepherds, in which blue eyes are common; in these instances, the level of dark pigment remains low, producing the blue "effect."

To put it another way: The color blue is not *inherent* in the eye—there's no blue pigment—but a function of the way it's "singled out" from the spectrum of visible light.

Why do puppies have such sharp teeth?

"My, what sharp teeth you have!" exclaimed Little Red Riding Hood to the Big Bad Wolf, who you'll recall was posing as Red's grandmother at the time. Dogs, of course, are essentially domesticated wolves—their DNA is all but identical—and perhaps the single biggest thing we can do to help make sense of our dogs, their behaviors, and their physical and psychological characteristics is to keep this wolfy ancestry in mind. As I like to put it: scratch a dog, find a wolf.

The teeth of puppies offer a prime example. When you think about the conditions in which a female wolf raises her pups, it becomes pretty obvious that their needle-sharp choppers, which begin to come in at around three weeks of age, serve a variety of critically important purposes. One is that they facilitate weaning. We all have nipples, and if you can imagine those tiny daggers clamping down on yours... well, I think you get the point. Once intense pain becomes part of the equation, Mama Wolf's ready to kick 'em out the door, where they can begin the process of learning to fend for themselves. (Too bad there isn't as powerful an incentive for human mothers to give the boot to their slacker, video game-addicted offspring.) By the same token, the weanling wolf needs good teeth in order to feed on the prey animals (or pieces of animals) that its dam retrieves to the den. Because the pup lacks size and strength, its teeth have to be that much sharper in order for it to tear off chunks of meat. By the time it cuts its adult teeth at six months of age, this is no longer an issue. The adult teeth also have to last a lifetime, so they're necessarily sturdier and less bayonet-like.

All of which is to say that the reason puppies have such sharp teeth is because they proved useful to their wild ancestors in the struggle for survival.

What Happens to Puppy Teeth When They Fall Out?

This is one of those questions that mystifies dog owners. Your little bundle of canine joy is teething, chewing on anything and everything it can get its jaws around as it rids itself of its puppy teeth and cuts its new, permanent set. Often, while playing with your pup, you'll notice a tooth that's wobbly and on the verge of falling out. You'll turn your attention elsewhere for a few minutes, and the next thing you know there's an empty socket where the tooth used to be. The pup's been in the room with you the whole time, but despite going over the floor with the proverbial fine-toothed comb, the missing chopper is nowhere to be found. The pup wouldn't have swallowed it… would he?

Yes, he would. When you consider all the other stuff pups eat, much of it bigger and harder to swallow (rocks, pieces of wood, the list goes on), bolting a tooth's not much of a stretch. This is why so few teeth end up under puppy pillows, waiting for the doggy tooth fairy. (Am I the only one who envisions a white poodle wearing a golden tiara and a pink tutu?) All things must pass, as they say, and with only the rarest exceptions these swallowed teeth travel harmlessly through the alimentary canal, eased along by the gentle hand of peristaltic action.

Why are some puppies "runts?"

Everyone is familiar with the phrase "the runt of the litter," whether they've ever laid eyes on a litter of puppies or not. In canine legend, of course, the runt, after being passed over in favor of his larger, more promising littermates (and enduring all manner of cruel misfortunes), grows up to fight man-eating grizzlies and rescue avalanche victims from certain death. There may be a germ of truth to this stereotype. Some believe that the runt, because it has to fight harder to nurse and get its rightful share in general, develops an extra measure of tenacity and determination.

What makes a runt a runt? Often it's simply an expression of normal genetic variation—the luck of the draw, in other words. A few pups are larger, most are somewhere in the middle, and a few are smaller. This gets into semantics, and the question of whether the smallest pup in the litter is always, by definition, "the runt"— even if it's just fractionally smaller than its littermates—or if "runt" refers only to puppies that are conspicuously smaller than the rest. Be that as it may, another reason some puppies lag behind in the size derby is that, due to the placement of the placenta, they don't receive as much nourishment through their umbilical cord as their littermates do. Some puppies may be conceived later, too, giving their littermates what amounts to a head start. It may take a while, but these pups usually catch up and develop normally.

Some runts, however, owe their small size to a serious underlying medical condition. This is why, if you have your heart set on the runt of the litter, you should be sure that it appears healthy and shows no signs of abnormal behavior (extreme timidity, for example), and have it thoroughly examined by a vet before any money changes hands.

Why are some litters very uniform in size and appearance while others are all over the place?

It's an amazing thing, the way the puppies in one litter will resemble the proverbial peas in a pod, while the puppies in another litter suggest the vegetable medley: peas, carrots, corn, green beans, maybe even some broccoli and cauliflower. Generally speaking, though, the more alike in size and appearance the parents, the more uniform in size and appearance the pups. At the risk of mixing metaphors, the apple doesn't fall far from the tree. In this same vein, purebred litters tend to be more uniform than mixed-breed litters, because what makes purebreds purebreds is that much of the variability has been weeded out in favor of specific characteristics that have been "fixed" over time by selective breeding. The result is what biologists call *homozygosity*, which is a fancy way of saying that dogs of the same breed have similar genetic material. Breed two Labradors, and their pups won't look like Schnauzers. This effect is intensified when you breed within an established bloodline, a practice known as linebreeding or, in a more extreme form, inbreeding. The legendary Elhew pointers, a strain cultivated for over 60 years by the late Robert G. Wehle, were perhaps the apotheosis of this, breeding "true to type" generation after generation.

Mate dogs of different breeds, however, and all bets are off. Now you're dealing with *heterozygosity*, which basically means that the gene pool resembles one of those frat house concoctions in which everyone brings a bottle and pours it into the bathtub. You never know what you'll get—which is why a single litter can have wildly different looking pups.

Why do puppies chew virtually *everything*?

Dogs of all ages are hard-wired to chew. In the wild (remember: scratch a dog, find a wolf), chewing on bones not only enabled the dog's ancestors to reap the nutritional benefit of every last molecule of protein but helped keep their teeth and gums healthy as well. Better health translates into a better chance to survive, which translates into a better chance to procreate… and in the evolutionary long run chewing became one of the definitive behaviors of the entire canine race.

Puppies, of course, chew for the added reason that it facilitates teething. The worst of it (from the standpoint of the typical homeowner, I mean) usually occurs when they're shedding their puppy teeth and cutting their permanent set. During this period, which begins at around three months of age and culminates at six to seven months, pups literally chew *everything*. The legs of wooden furniture are a favored target—they tend to be at puppy level, for one thing, and the wood has a pleasing "mouth feel"—along with electrical cords, shoes and slippers (leather is as irresistible to puppies as beer nuts are to barflies), stuffed animals, pillows, rugs, the list goes on (and on).

Another reason puppies chew is the sheer thrill of finding out what they can do with them. It's no different when we get a new toy, or suddenly discover an aptitude, such as playing a musical instrument or whacking 300-yard drives, that we didn't know we possessed. Boredom tends to exacerbate problem chewing, and it also tends to be more prevalent in breeds like Labs and goldens that seem to have an innate need to use their mouths, whether for good, i.e., retrieving, or evil, i.e., shredding everything in sight.

Why do puppies love to bite one another on the ears and the back of the neck?

The term "rough and tumble" might have been coined with puppies in mind. It certainly describes their world to the proverbial T, filled as it is with surprise attacks, tag-team wrestling matches, and tussles of every description. Sometimes a clear victor emerges, but more often the pups simply collapse as one under the weight of their exertions, wobbling like drunks for a moment or two before passing out as instantaneously and comprehensively as if they'd been conked on the head with a sap.

In the same way that the Battle of Waterloo was won on the playing fields of Eton, as Lord Wellington famously observed, "play fighting" prepares puppies to handle themselves in the cold, cruel world. (It was a lot more important when dogs were still wolves, but deep inside every dog there's a voice telling it not to take its next meal for granted.) It helps them develop coordination, motor skills, and overall physical soundness, and it also nurtures confidence and independence. As far as why the ears and the back of the neck absorb the brunt of the punishment, I think it's largely a matter of opportunity: they're soft, they're easy to get a good grip on, and while the "recipient" may scream bloody murder the chances of actually drawing blood are remote. In fact, I have a hunch that one of the reasons puppies gravitate to these areas is precisely *because* they're resistant to injury—nature's way of letting the little buggers have at it tooth and nail without doing any lasting harm. Play fighting also teaches puppies how to control their biting behavior, so they can later hold in reserve for only the direst emergencies.

Why do some puppies bully their littermates?

Well, because some puppies *are* bullies, the way some kids are. (Some adults are bullies, too, of course, including more than a few with addresses in Washington, D.C.) And just as two-legged bullies swagger, posture, cow their subordinates, and assert their real or imagined superiority at every opportunity, the four-legged kind take a snarky delight in lording over their littermates. They push their brothers and sisters around, commandeering their food, water, and toys and making it clear that what the others do have is only at the pleasure of the Tough Guy.

Unlike human bullies, however, whose behavior is typically explained by deep-rooted feelings of inferiority (if not by an intransigent meanness straight out of Cormac McCarthy), canine bullying is ultimately an expression of dominance aimed at establishing one's place in the hierarchy of the pack—although the worst bullies, ironically, are generally not the alpha dogs themselves but the alpha "wannabes," the pups whose reach exceeds their grasp. So it could be that an element of inferiority drives this behavior after all. Sometimes, too, a mild-mannered pup that's been quietly taking it from the bully will reach its breaking point, retaliate with startling fury, and in an instant re-shuffle the whole nascent pack dynamic. You know what they say: It's not the size of the dog in the fight, but the size of the fight in the dog.

Why do puppies make "play" growls but not "mean" growls? When do the "mean" growls start?

Of the many puppy behaviors guaranteed to prompt a bemused chuckle, the "puppy growl" has to be near the top of the list. It's just so incongruous to hear this mock-ferocious sound issue from such a tiny, cuddly, utterly unthreatening source—something like being in the audience when a petite singer like Mariah Carey or Martina McBride takes the stage, opens her mouth, and all but blows the roof off. You wonder, 'Where the heck did *that* come from?'

Puppy growls are part-and-parcel of the whole "play fighting" ritual, the process by which puppies learn their capabilities in combat and, just as importantly, learn to control and inhibit them. The function of growling, in fact, is not merely to serve as a warning, but as a deterrent; in the wild, where these behaviors evolved and were incorporated into the dog's genetic blueprint, there's very little survival value in scrapping over every bone of contention. And while the pup doing the growling undoubtedly thinks he (or she) means business, puppy growls clearly lack the menacing tone of "mean" growls, the kind that make the hair on the back of your neck stand up, to say nothing of the hair on the backs of any dogs in the vicinity. Dogs will indulge in occasional bouts of play fighting throughout their lives (those that live as house- or kennel-mates in particular), but among littermates the play fighting period starts winding down at about 11 weeks of age and is pretty much over by 15 weeks. After that, the growls tend to have teeth in them.

Why are puppies born "deaf"?

Essentially, it's for the same reason that they're born "blind." (And yes, I know they're not really born deaf—although some puppies are—but it gets a little tiresome saying "born unable to hear because their ear canals are closed.") Over the eons, the strategy that worked best for the wolf's survival, and therefore became integral to the dog's genetic make-up, was a gestation period of about two months followed by a two-week "neo-natal" period during which many features of the puppies' physiology undergo critical development—development that the young of more precocious species (the large hooved mammals, for example) undergo while still in the womb.

A certain amount of sensory deprivation is an important part of this process. Just as the puppy's eyelids are fused shut to protect the nascent optic structures until they're ready to respond to light, the pup's ear canals are sealed closed, thus preventing sound waves from entering and "activating" the fragile auditory machinery until it, too, is capable of handling the stimulus. Unlike the sense of sight, however, which starts out at a very rudimentary level and grows in acuity over the weeks that follow, the puppy's sense of hearing is quite acute as soon as the ear canals fully open.

Why do puppies' mothers clean up after them for the first few weeks—and why do they stop?

One of the measures of how helpless puppies are at birth—and how utterly reliant they are on their mothers—is that they can't even defecate or urinate on their own. Instead, by licking their anuses and uro-genital openings, the puppies' dam stimulates them to poop and pee. This continues for approximately two to three weeks, when the pups, despite their wobbly legs, begin "taking care of business" by themselves. During this same neo-natal period and for some time beyond, the mother also cleans up after her puppies, dutifully hoovering their soft, relatively odorless (or at least not terribly *mal*odorous) stools. This is nature's way of keeping the whelping and brooding area clean, thus minimizing its attraction both to parasites and potential predators. In that place deep in the dog's psyche where the wolf still howls, mama wants her nest to be as inconspicuous as possible.

Once the pups start eating solid food, though, their stools become unpalatable and the dam grows increasingly disinclined to "police the area." This has the effect of kick-starting the weaning process, and as milk comprises an ever-smaller percentage of the pups' diet the bitch produces less and less of it until she finally "dries up." The pups, in turn, are forced to become more independent and assert their individuality—putting them in just the right place, psychologically, to start new lives with their human pack.

Why do puppies "spin" like wind-up toys?

In a way, this question has it backwards. It seems entirely likely to me that, in yet another instance of art imitating life, spinning puppies were the inspiration that caused wind-up toys to be invented in the first place. It would be closer to the truth, then, to say that wind-up toys spin like puppies.

So why do puppies spin? Because they're so excited, so exuberantly joyful, so overcome by the delirious thrill of living and the possibilities of their existence that, if they could, they'd come right out of their skins. They literally don't know what to do with themselves, but somehow, someway, they have to move. It's like the way some people just have to dance when they hear Tina Turner sing "Proud Mary." Another factor that influences and even conditions pups to spin (as opposed to racing back-and-forth, another common expression of youthful exuberance) is that they're in a relatively small space—the whelping pen, for example. Their options are limited, and spinning gives them the biggest bang for their buck. There's a demonstrative aspect as well. Having learned to associate people with good things—food, play, etc.—there's a sense in which the pups spin for *you*. And even older dogs will spin circles in anticipation of suppertime, going for a walk, or some other pleasant experience.

A certain amount of happy, situational spinning is normal—but chronic, excessive spinning is often the sign of a pup that's spent too much time confined to a crate and is poorly socialized in general. It can also be symptomatic of a serious underlying neurological condition—epilepsy, to name one—so if your pup's spinning to a degree that causes concern, a visit to the veterinarian is definitely in order.

Why does puppy breath smell so sweet?

The mere fact that you're reading this means you're a puppy-lover, so I really shouldn't have to convince you that puppy breath is an exhalation of such divine and wondrous subtlety that there is literally nothing to compare it to. It's a kind of vaporous nectar, a misty swirl of milk and honey, and you don't smell it so much as you drink it, savoring every draught to the last delicious molecule. It's addictive, narcotic, and if you need further proof just Google "puppy breath." What you'll find is a vast community of zealots, ordained by the force of their beliefs to extol the miracle that is puppy breath and share it with the rest of the world. It's a bit alarming, really.

The reason puppy breath smells the way it does—sweet but not cloyingly so, like a warm summer breeze wafting through a peach orchard—is that the puppy's diet of mother's milk, along with the enzymes that break it down, combine in what can only be described as alchemy. The result is singular—and magical. But it is also, like puppyhood itself, ephemeral. As the puppy is weaned and milk comprises an ever-smaller percentage of its diet, its breath gradually changes to, well, dog breath. By the time the pup's three months of age, the breath that made you want to hold it to your face at every opportunity has all but vanished. It's not that dog breath's bad, necessarily (although the breath of a dog with periodontal disease or a throat abcess will send you reeling), it's just that the only dogs with good breath tend to be yours. Funny how that works.

Why do puppies have that special "puppy smell"?

Like the aroma of baking bread, or the scent of cotton sheets hung out to dry on the first warm day of spring, puppies have a smell that's all their own—and that's hard to get enough of. A certain portion of this is attributable to the phenomenon of "puppy breath" which, if it could be distilled, bottled, and sold would make some entrepreneur very, very rich. Another factor is the fastidious grooming performed by the puppy's mother, who starts licking them as soon as they exit the birth canal—it's pretty comical to watch a tiny newborn pup get rolled across the whelping box like a bocce ball—and maintains this practice until they're well on their way to being weaned. (You'd smell good, too, if you had someone willing to bathe you every three or four hours.) It's also the case that, in somewhat the same way that teenage kids begin having skin problems when they reach puberty, the oily secretions called *sebum* don't fully kick in until around six months of age (it varies from breed to breed), when the pup begins to shed its "puppy coat" and grow in its adult coat. These secretions, which are produced by glands in the hair follicles and are what give the coat its gloss and sheen, are the primary source of "dog smell," at least as far as the dull olfactory powers of humans are concerned. Other dogs, of course, find the scent emitted by their brethren's anal sacs to be much more instructive.

In any event, enjoy your puppy's smell while you can, because it'll be gone before you can say "Get off the couch!"

Why do retrieving breed puppies retrieve at a very early age?

The old professional trainer was putting on a brave front, but we both knew he was nearing the end of the line. Now, as he shuffled toward a dusty shelf in the dimly lit kennel building, a pair of weanling Labrador retriever pups—one yellow, one black—nipped at his pants legs. He found a puppy-sized dummy to which he'd duct-taped a pair of pigeon wings, waved it in the youngsters' faces to get their attention, and tossed it down the hallway. The floppy-eared pups, still at that age when they seem to have more skin than they can fill, scrabbled after it. The yellow one got there first, and without missing a beat she grabbed the dummy, turned around, and *brought it back*. The old trainer beamed—and the years fell away. Through the simple act of retrieving, a pudgy little puppy had given an old man reason enough to carry on. Perhaps she had not made him young again, but she'd helped him to remember how it felt.

What made this magic possible? Selective breeding—generation upon generation of it. By choosing sires and dams who exhibit a strong natural inclination to retrieve, and repeating this process over literally dozens of generations and hundreds of years, the retrieving instinct has been intensified until it burns in the Lab, the golden, and the Chesapeake like the focused blue flame of a welder's torch. It's their dominant, defining characteristic; they're never happier than when they're retrieving, and they'll pester you unmercifully to get you to throw something—*anything*—for them to fetch. They can't help it; they were born that way.

Why do pointing breed puppies "sight point" at a very early age?

It never fails to produce "oohs," "aahs," and "wows"—an entire litter of pudgy, shoebox-sized puppies frozen in their tracks, their tails rigid (as rigid as they can make them, anyway) and their expressions deadly serious as they sight-point a robin, or a butterfly, or, most likely, a pheasant, grouse, or quail wing flicked from an old fishing rod. Although it doesn't have to be a wing—a white handkerchief, or anything else that gets and keeps the pups' attention, works just as well—the "wing on a string" is a time-honored tool for assessing a puppy's pointing instinct. A pup that readily locks up on the wing is said to have "a lot of point," and is generally considered a better, more precocious prospect than a pup that just wants to chase it. Many experienced dog people are also convinced that the style and intensity a puppy displays while pointing a wing accurately predict the style and intensity it will display as an adult.

This is one of those behaviors that's directly attributable to hundreds of years of selective breeding. First the point itself, which has its roots in the stalk common to all mammalian predators, was isolated and "fixed"—a process that began as early as the 13th century. Then, as it was continually refined and reinforced, it became the dominant, definitive behavior of the pointer (the acknowledged top dog in this respect), the setters, and, to a somewhat lesser extent, the other pointing breeds. Some pups start pointing by the time they're three weeks old—as soon as their legs work and their eyes are open, basically.

Why do puppies get the hiccups?

Most of us have had the experience, notoriously re-created in an episode of *Seinfeld*, of being introduced by beaming parents to their newborn pride-and-joy… and recoiling in shock at the face peeking up from the crib. This is when the ability to display "grace under pressure," in Hemingway's famous formulation, goes a long way.

Happily, we don't have to worry about this with puppies. They can be sort of lumpy and amorphous, even amoeboid, during their first few weeks of life, but they're never unappealing. Something that puppies and babies *do* have in common, though, is that they both get the hiccups. Getting the hiccups is natural and normal—kind of endearing in fact (human babies even get hiccups *in utero*)—and while eating, drinking, and general excitement can sometimes trigger an "attack" there's often no discernible rhyme or reason to them. The good news is that they tend to pass just as quickly and unaccountably as they started—and no, you should not try to "scare" the hiccups out of a puppy, or for that matter attempt any of the other home remedies that your mom may have inflicted on you when it seemed your hiccups would never subside. Most puppies outgrow the hiccups by the time they're eight months old or so, and while an older dog will occasionally get them there seems to be no record of canine hiccups lasting for years and even decades, as has been documented in humans. As for the question of why hiccups happen in the first place, there's some speculation that they may have originally aided in dislodging food that was "stuck," but the bottom line is that no one really knows.

Why do puppies sleep on their backs?

Whether '70s punk-rock pioneers The Ramones originated the phrase or merely appropriated it for their album of the same name, "bop 'til you drop" has become part of the American vernacular. ("Shop 'til you drop" came later, presumably.) And while certain nuances of meaning tend to be lost in translation, it basically means to keep going at full speed until your legs can't support you any more and you literally collapse on the spot from exhaustion. If this m.o. sounds familiar, it's because it describes puppies, up to the age of three or four months or so to the proverbial T. They go, and go, and go until, as you watch with a growing smile, they wobble, totter, and fall. You're tempted to holler "Timber!"

So it's not so much that they specifically sleep on their backs as it is that they sleep—soundly, comfortably, and deeply—in whatever position, and in whatever location they happen to be in. This is an ability that many Americans, by all accounts the world's most troubled sleepers, can only envy (as they reach for their Ambien). Some adult dogs occasionally sleep on their backs as well, which is if anything an even more comical sight than the puppy version. Come to think of it, all the adult dogs I've known to sleep on their backs were males. I suppose this could be evidence of a streak of exhibitionism, but I'll let you draw your own conclusions.

Why do puppies sleep in a pile?

For the same reason that you snuggle under the blankets with your honey on a cold winter's night: warmth. (If you were thinking of something else, you must be a newlywed.) Puppies in their "neo-natal" stage—their first two weeks or life, roughly—lack the ability to regulate or maintain their core temperature, which gradually rises from about 97°F at birth to the "normal" 101°F at about three weeks of age. They're completely dependent on their environment for warmth during this period; conversely, they're extremely susceptible to cold. This is the reason conscientious breeders always provide some kind of supplemental heat source to the whelping pen. A heated pad is one popular option (with care taken to see it doesn't get too hot); another is a heat lamp suspended—at a safe remove, obviously—over the puppies' "nest." It doesn't have to be like a sauna—there's the puppies' mama to consider, too—but it should be on the upper side of comfortable.

Of course, the closest and most accessible sources of heat in the environment of a typical puppy are its littermates, hence the familiar "pile o' pups" as one after the other crawls, climbs, and worms his or her way onto the stack. It's sort of the same principle that we use when we create a nice, neat mound of charcoal briquets preparatory to carbonizing a perfectly good piece of beef. Truth be told, though, these puppy pile-ups can be an indication that the ambient temperature's a bit too low, forcing the pups to go to extremes to conserve warmth.

Why do puppies sometimes cry out even when nothing's wrong?

The kicker here is the qualifier "even when nothing's wrong." While there may be nothing *obviously* wrong— the puppy's not hungry, or cold, or being tormented by a littermate, or in a strange environment away from its mama, its siblings, and everything it's ever known—you have to remember that a young puppy is learning as it goes. With just about every moment that passes (every conscious one, anyway) it's exposed to new sensations and stimuli. A little puppy has essentially zero "life experience," and as a result everything comes as a surprise to it, sometimes so much so that the pup's startled into crying out. It could be a growl emanating from its own stomach, the bubble of a burp rising in its esophagus, a gassy twinge in its bowels, or just some neuron firing randomly and unexpectedly.

It could be something external, too, such as a noise (even one that doesn't strike us as loud), flipping on a light— literally anything, from within or without, that the puppy doesn't know what to make of, or that upsets its delicate status quo. Certainly some puppies are innately more "reactive" than others; it's one of the breeder's jobs to raise the pups in the kind of nurturing, stimulating environment that provides them with the confidence and "social skills" to adapt to new situations, overcome its fears, and ameliorate any neurotic tendencies. The last thing any breeder wants is to have a puppy from his/her kennel become one of Cesar Millan's case studies.

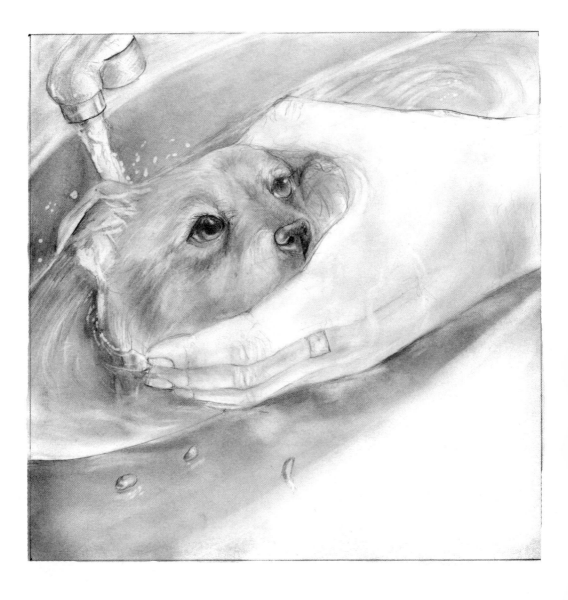

Why do puppies dislike being held under water so much?

Just so everybody's clear on this, we're not talking about submersion a la some sort of baptismal ritual—you know, one of those scenes out of Faulkner or Flannery O'Connor where a sinner wades into the river, gets dunked by the preacher, and comes up sputtering "I'm saved!" (At least I *hope* that's not what we're talking about; the questions that comprise this book were solicited from the author's wide circle of acquaintances in the dog world—breeders, veterinarians, enthusiasts of every stripe—and it's possible that some of them have frames of reference with which I'm unfamiliar.) What we mean, instead, is why do puppies dislike being shampooed, having the mud hosed off of them, stuff like that.

Well, if you'll forgive me for putting the answer in the form of another question:

Have you ever known a kid who willingly submitted to taking a bath? It's not that puppies dislike water; on the contrary, assuming it's not ice-cold or scalding-hot, most puppies love splashing, swimming, and generally whooping it up in it. What they don't like is being held in place and having water *forced* on them. It's an affront to their dignity, a blow to their pride. Plus, like literally everything else they experience during puppyhood, it's something they have to get used to. Feeling all that water cascading over them, especially as it works through their coat and onto their skin, has got to be a pretty unnerving sensation for a pup with nothing to compare it to. But then, my wife, who's—oh, let's leave her age out of it—can't stand the way water jetted from a shower feels on her skin, either.

Why are puppies rarely afraid of new people but usually suspicious of new dogs?

It comes back, as it so often does with puppies, to socialization. Puppies that have been handled, played with, and fussed over, preferably by more than one person and ideally by children (kids and puppies truly are a match made in heaven), tend to show little if any fear of new people. Assuming they've had nothing but pleasant experiences in human company, they have no reason to view people as threats. And it points up the reason why, if you're looking over a litter of puppies as a prospective buyer, it's a good rule of thumb to steer clear of any pups that *do* seem unusually timid. Whatever the underlying cause (and I realize this sounds a bit flinty), it's probably not something you want to deal with—unless you're going in with your eyes wide open, fully aware that you're taking on a "project."

New dogs, however, are a different story. In the first place, most pups will have little if any exposure to other dogs (excepting their dam and littermates) until sometime after they've been weaned. So they're not as habituated to dogs as they are to humans, and less trustful of them as a result. But something deeper is at work, too, something with roots reaching back thousands of years to a time when the dog's ancestors lived by the rule of the fang and the claw, and survival meant accepting nothing at face value. Simply put, puppies are instinctively wary of other dogs, and will keep their guard up around them until they've been thoroughly vetted and their motives deemed sincere. It's the way of the pack, the dog's wolf progenitors having learned the hard way that those most like you are in the best position to do you harm.

Why do puppies always want to get to your face?

One of the keys to understanding canine behavior is that the dog's primary means of taking in the world around it is its sense of smell. What makes this a difficult concept for us to wrap our minds around is that we, too, have a sense of smell, and we naturally try to put ourselves in our dogs' place by imagining what it would be like if ours was better. Except it doesn't work that way; our imaginations aren't that good. The dog's nose is so vastly superior to ours, so much more powerful and discerning, that it might as well be a different organ entirely, one that allows the dog to operate in a realm of perception that's utterly closed to us. The only legitimate comparison—the only one that frames the discussion in truly meaningful terms—is between the dog's sense of smell and our sense of sight. This is why I like to say that dogs *see with their noses.*

The same goes for puppies. In fact, it's tempting to speculate that, within the intricate calculus of evolution, one of the reasons puppies are born blind and deaf is that it forces them to rely on their noses first, foremost, and forever. The reason they love to get to our faces, then, is that they can drink in the incredible bouquet of aromas emanating from our mouths (and clinging to our lips, mustaches, etc.). It's a curious thing about dogs that they appear to enjoy our breath—morning breath, beer breath, it doesn't seem to matter—and if that doesn't illustrate the fact that they smell things a whole lot differently than we do, I don't know what does.

Why will puppies run right to you if you sit down?

It's Canine Behavior 101: If you want a dog to come to you, you need to get down to its level. Dogs, even puppies, are acutely aware of body language, which they interpret in the hierarchical terms of the pack: dominance, submission, subordination, and so on. By getting down to their level—squatting, sitting, even merely bending down—you're eliminating the perceived barriers and telling the pups that you're their equal, which in the puppy world-view is like getting an invitation to a birthday party with all the cake and ice cream you can eat. The pups' natural inquisitiveness kicks in, too—*Hey, check this out!*—and they're on you in a heartbeat, climbing, jumping, licking, furiously wagging their tails, acting like they're ants and you're a hill that's been smeared with honey.

Of course, once puppies learn how much fun it is to crawl all over you—once the behavior is reinforced, that is, by your willingness to play with them and the obvious delight you take in the game—you become a marked man. They'll seize any opportunity, take advantage of the flimsiest excuse to mob, maul, and otherwise gang up on you. And you'll love it, not only because it's so much fun you expect the cops to show up at any moment but because it means you've raised the puppies right.

Why will puppies leave their mother in an instant for any kid that happens by?

As chronicled in countless novels, stories, and memoirs—Willie Morris's unforgettable My Dog Skip, to name one—kids and dogs share something that adults can only look upon with envy (and, if they're lucky, nostalgia, having enjoyed that special relationship when they were young themelves). Having a dog when you're a kid is like being given the keys to the kingdom, and whether it was magical or not at the time, that's the way we invariably remember it—especially as we grow older.

It starts in puppyhood, typically. Puppies look at kids—which is to say, they size them up and smell them over— and instinctively recognize them as kin. They're soulmates, *simpatico*, bursting with the same curiosity and thirst for knowledge, the same zest for life and innocent, uncomplicated approach to living. It's as if they have an elemental connection, as if they know, with a deep-in-the-gut certainty, that they belong together. Puppies seem to know that kids are up for any adventure, too, which fits paw-in-glove with the canine race's inborn need for "voyaging," as Elizabeth Marshall Thomas put it in her acclaimed *The Hidden Life of Dogs*. And so a puppy, given half a chance, will always fall in with a kid, trotting alongside with a look that seems to say "OK, Boss, what's on the agenda today?" They simply understand that kids are their perfect companions, which makes complete sense when you consider that they've had at least 15,000 years to figure it out.

Why do puppies "go limp" when you pick them up?

It's an amazing transformation: the way a puppy that seems to be everywhere at once, a bright-eyed bundle of crackling kinetic energy—and a mischievous one at that—goes as limp as overcooked linguine the moment you pick it up. This is about as predictable, on the face of it, as mild-mannered Bruce Banner turning into the raging Incredible Hulk (or vice-versa).

What the heck's going on here? Well, we've all seen video of wild canids—wolves, coyotes, foxes—picking up their young by the scruff of the neck and retrieving them back to the den, relocating them to a safer location, and/or keeping them out of harm's way in general. Garnished with an emphatic shake, this is also how the mama administers discipline and asserts her authority. Over the millennia, canid puppies have evolved to recognize being picked up or shaken as "cues" to give in and submit—to take their medicine, you might say. In the long run (the only race that matters in the evolutionary Olympics), more of the pups that displayed such behavior survived—as opposed to those that struggled and "fought it"—and after many generations the "limp response" became part of the canine race's genetic make-up. It tends to diminish over time, of course, with the youngest pups displaying it to the strongest degree and the "adolescents" reacting like teenagers (which is what they are, essentially), being docile one moment and having a hissy fit the next.

Why do puppies make grown men fall to their knees and make baby talk?

Speaking for myself, I don't recall making "baby talk" to puppies. I have my own special puppy dialect, which comes out sounding like a Tibetan Buddhist chant uttered in a sing-song Southern drawl. As far as falling to my knees and pretty much turning into mush whenever I get around a litter of pups, though, I take a back seat to none. Been there, done that, as they say—and with any luck I'll be doing it until there's a serious question as to whether I can get *off* my knees once I've fallen on them.

Nothing strips away the façade of adulthood and reveals—or maybe restores—the boy inside the man the way puppies do. They make us young again; they remind us that we take ourselves much too seriously and that many of the things we obsessively worry about aren't really that important. If you want to say they put things in perspective, I won't disagree. They embody such carefree innocence and optimism, and display their emotions so nakedly and guilelessly, that we have to envy them. Their needs are simple; they have no hidden agendas, no ulterior motives. They say "Pick me, and in return for whatever you can spare, even if it's just the crumbs from your table, I will give you my undying love and loyalty, my infinite empathy and boundless compassion, my patient wisdom and fierce devotion. All of it, forever." It's the best deal we ever made—and it's why, when that certain puppy's eyes meet yours, you can throw all books and articles on "how to pick the perfect puppy" right out the window. You just know.

Why does it take some puppies so long to outgrow their desire to nurse?

A woman I know, very much in the "Earth Mother" mold, nursed her babies until they could walk, talk, and darn near tie their own shoes. It never got quite to where they were saying "Mother, may I?," but it was always a little disconcerting when one of her kids toddled up, wagged a pudgy pink finger at her chest, and, in an imperiously demanding tone, said "Nam-nam."

The point is that children will continue to nurse for as long as they're given the opportunity. There's no magical date, or age, at which the desire suddenly vanishes; what happens is that it becomes inconvenient for mom, and so she shuts down the operation. The same goes for puppies. Their attitude is: If the dairy bar's open, why not belly up to it? This is why puppies that have been weaned and separated from their dam will, if turned out in the yard with her, invariably try to "latch on" and steal a few pulls from the tap. They're doing what comes naturally to them; it's how they're wired. Their dam, who by now has had quite enough of this—and who is acutely aware of the fact that her brood are now sporting their needle-sharp puppy teeth—will try to avoid them at first, and if that doesn't work she'll put them in their place with a growl and a good "scruffing." The persistence that certain pups display in attempting to nurse can be explained in several ways. It could be that they're hungrier, and it could be that they're more tenacious in general. Mostly, though, it's just a function of the usual "bell curve" variation, with the behavior exhibited by the few at either end framing and defining the "normal" behavior of the majority in the middle.

Why do puppies need vaccinations?

All puppies receive a measure of immunity from their dams. Think of it as a "starter kit." It shields them from diseases like distemper and parvovirus for the first several weeks of their lives, but it's strictly temporary—and as it wears off the pups need a helping hand to fire up their own immune systems and get the antibody production line rolling. That, essentially, is what vaccinations do.

While puppies acquire some immunity *in utero* through the placenta, the larger portion is delivered via the colostrum, the protein- and nutrient-rich "first milk" produced within 24 hours of whelping. The colostrum is packed with antibodies, and only within the first few hours of its life is the puppy able to absorb these large protein molecules "whole"—without having to break them

into smaller pieces, that is—thus retaining their disease-fighting properties. All else equal, the higher the dam's level of immunity, the more antibodies she'll pass to her pups—and the higher their level of immunity as a result. The kicker with maternal immunity is that it's "passive," meaning that it lasts only as long as the antibodies she gave her puppies last. As they erode over time, the puppies' immunity weakens.

Unfortunately, this loss of maternal immunity is necessary in order for vaccines to do their job and stimulate the puppy's "active," self-replenishing immunity. So there's still a period, known as the window of susceptibility, when puppies are in a kind of immunological limbo, their maternal immunity too weak to protect them from disease but too strong to permit the vaccines to kick in. This is why parvovirus, for example, still claims a few victims every year.

So Why Do Puppies Get Worms?

While it's possible for older puppies to pick up parasitic intestinal worms from their environment—the same way adult dogs get them, basically—it's a curious fact that many if not most puppies are born with the common dog roundworm, *Toxocara canis*. The pups typically contract the worms *in utero*, although in some cases they're born "clean" only to ingest the parasites through their mother's milk. What makes this puzzling is that their dams may well have tested negative for worms prior to breeding, or been on a medication regimen that made the test moot. (Most heartworm preventatives these days also knock out roundworms and one or two other varieties of intestinal parasite.)

So what gives? Well, if the dam has ever had roundworms, and chances are she has—it just goes with the territory if you're a dog—some of them have in all likelihood migrated from the intestinal tract and "encysted" in the liver or muscle tissues. Undetectable, untreatable, and causing no harm to their host in their encysted state, they can remain dormant for years. Re-activated by pregnancy, however, some of the worms—actually the microscopic larvae—migrate through the uterus and placenta to the puppies. Other larvae find their way to the female's mammary glands, where they enter the milk and are ingested by the nursing pups. This is why you can have a dam in perfect health and a whelping box so clean even Monk couldn't find fault with it, yet your puppies can still have worms. This is also why competent, scrupulous breeders "de-worm" their puppies as a matter of course.

Why do puppies love to eat poop?

It's not just puppies. I used to have a pointer, Traveler, who had the jowly mien of a pensioned British military officer. My wife called him "Colonel Mustard." You could easily imagine him clearing his throat and harrumphing, "When I was with Gordon in Khartoum…" But here's the thing—whenever he thought he could get away with it, this dignified-looking canine aristocrat would sneak into the basement and raid the litter box. I remember one incident in particular when, having caught him in the act and roared my displeasure, I heard my 10-year-old stepdaughter casually remark to her mother, "Uh-oh, Traveler's eating cat poop again."

Some puppies outgrow this behavior—the technical term for which, by the way, is *coprophagy*—and some, like Traveler, never do. The range of dishes on the fecal menu is impressive, too, from cow pies and horse apples to the scat of various wild critters (rabbit pellets are all but irresistible) to the stools of other dogs and even (gak!) their own. Obviously, the stuff doesn't taste bad to them, and the reason it doesn't is that the dog's wolf forebears, faced with the alternative of starving to death when the pickings were slim in their hunting territories, adapted to scarf pretty much anything with nutritive value—including, if necessary, turds. Anxiety, stress, and boredom are sometimes associated with coprophagy in older dogs, as is the desire to simply "cover their tracks." In puppies, though, curiosity probably has as much to do with it as anything. If they can fit it in their mouths, they'll try to eat it.

79

Why do some puppies never seem to grow up?

A word you see a lot these days is *ethology*, which is the branch of zoology concerned with the study of animal behavior and how it relates to genetics, evolution, anatomy, and physiology. It's a relatively recent discipline (although its roots are ancient), and it's no coincidence that one of its founders was Konrad Lorenz, whose *Man Meets Dog*, first published in 1954, remains one of the most influential books ever written on the subject of canine behavior and the principles of training. After all, what animal does man have a longer or more intimate relationship with than the dog?

And a word that ethologists use a lot when they're talking about dogs—and in particular when they're describing the process by which the dog split off from the wolf, was domesticated, and essentially *became* the dog—is *neoteny*. Neoteny refers to the retention of juvenile characteristics into adulthood, and most ethologists believe it's the critical "wedge" that separated the dog from the wolf and endowed it with the qualities that make it both useful and beloved—the qualities that make dogs dogs and not wolves, in other words. The upshot is that dogs never entirely grow up; psychologically, they keep one paw in puppyhood their entire lives. This is why they remain playful, affectionate, and eager-to-please, and this is also why they remain trainable. The really irrepressible, happy-go-lucky types just have more Peter Pan in them than most.

Why do puppies urinate when they get excited?

It's happened to everyone. We get home, the new puppy joyfully bounds to greet us—and suddenly there's a suspicious puddle on the kitchen floor. Hey, better there than on our shoes, right? "Excitement urination," this is called, and as the term implies it's simply a matter of the puppy—who's still developing, still learning how to use his muscles and respond to stimuli—getting so jazzed that he loses control of his bladder. If you've ever laughed so hard you nearly peed your pants, you can identify with that. It's completely normal (if a bit inconvenient), and the vast majority of puppies outgrow it by the time they're about six months old. A pup that continues to "piddle," though, should be checked over by a vet, as it could be suffering from an infection or a congenital defect that makes it difficult to hold its urine.

One thing you should never do is reprimand a pup for this behavior. It's not the pup's fault—he literally can't help it—and other than giving the pup ample opportunity to relieve itself in the appropriate location and trying to control the situation so he doesn't get over-excited there's not much you can, or should, do. Scolding a pup for excitement urination is just plain ignorant; plus, it can lead to "submissive urination," which is a display of deference and a way to apologize for whatever the pup may have done that, in its mind, you might have cause to be angry about. It can be hard to distinguish between the two—some urination episodes undoubtedly have elements of both—but submissive urination, because of the added psychological component, tends to be more problematic.

Why do puppies roll over on their backs when you approach them?

This is the classic example of submissive behavior and, again, it's not only puppies that display it. Whenever a dog of any age wants to send the clear message "I acknowledge you as my superior and yield to your dominance," it flops onto its back. What it's really doing, though, is exposing its most vulnerable, unprotected area, the proverbial "soft underbelly." For a predator species like the dog—and remember: Scratch a dog, find a wolf—this is a gesture of incredible symbolic power, a cue that dogs have evolved to respond to in prescribed ways. It signals acquiescence, immediately de-fuses potential violence, and resolves any disputes or disagreements within the hierarchy of the pack. In some cases, particularly when puppies are involved, this gesture is accompanied by urination, which is pretty comical unless you happen to be in the line of fire. (There is a legendary story about a golden retriever that did this at a big field trial, right in front of God and the gallery, when its handler gave it a command it didn't want to obey.)

Puppies being puppies, still feeling their way and finding their place in the world, this behavior tends to be more common among them. It's the "better safe than sorry" approach, and a pup's propensity to display it is a fairly accurate barometer of how compliant and agreeable it'll be when the serious training starts. Indeed, one of the "tests" often recommended for evaluating puppies is to hold them on their backs and see whether they struggle or give in. I've never put a lot of stock in it, but then, pretty much all my dogs have been knot-heads (although lovable ones).

Why will puppies pounce on anything that moves?

When you stop to think about it, this is very near the top of the list of things that make puppies so much fun to play with, especially when you include the chase that typically precedes the pounce. It's endlessly engrossing, not to mention just plain fun, to watch them go after bugs, butterflies, their littermates' tails, the list is endless. Part of the appeal is the way they assume that super-serious look when they're stalking their "prey"—as if they were diplomats trying to hammer out a disarmament treaty—a look that's incongruously (and charmingly) out of keeping with everything else about them.

In fact, "prey" is exactly the right metaphor. Dogs are predators—their DNA, remember, is only 0.2 percent different from the wolf's—and when something near them moves (in particular if it moves away from them, the way a prey animal would) it triggers what ethologists call the *prey chase drive*. It's instinctive, a hard-wired, automatic response that, especially in puppies, has yet to be reined in by experience, maturity, and training. It's indiscriminate, too, unfortunately, which is the reason dogs chase cars. Depending on the breed, the prey object, and the outcome of previous chases, the pup may throttle down and go into "stalk" mode, stealthily creeping up on its quarry and even momentarily pointing it. Then the puppy gathers itself, pounces—and, for its sake, better hope that the bumblebee gets away.

Why do light-colored puppies "tick out" and get darker with age?

It's always fun, with a litter of newborn pups, to play the guessing game of how they'll be marked when they grow up. In the case of breeds whose coats are predominantly white such as the pointer, English setter, English cocker, German shorthair, and Brittany, while their "masks" and larger patches of body color are typically visible right away, the $64,000 question is the extent to which their white background will fill in with ticking—the small, dot-like daubs of darker hue, usually black, liver, or orange, that give many dogs of these breeds their "speckled" look. If you're not prepared for this possibility—and there are plenty of inexperienced puppy buyers who aren't—it can come as a bit of a shock a few months down the road. Dogs that are very heavily ticked are referred to as "beltons"

(the term is primarily associated with English setters), while dogs in which darker hairs are evenly blended with lighter ones are known as "roans." White dogs that display little or no ticking or roaning are said to have an "open" coat.

If you're thinking this sounds awfully complicated, well, it is. The genetics of coat color inheritance are exceedingly complex—and at best imperfectly understood. (There are even bewildering correlations between certain coat colors and congenital health defects, deafness in particular, that show up in some breeds.) Suffice it to say that, in much the same way that most puppies' eyes start out blue and ultimately become some shade of brown, the reason that the coats of light-colored pups tend to darken over time is that it takes a while for their complete pigmentation to kick in.

Why do puppies sometimes run "sideways"?

You wonder if it's an optical illusion, the way a spoked tire can appear to be turning backwards, or if your eyes are just somehow playing tricks on you. Your puppy, who seems normal in every respect, is running—except instead of running the direction he's pointing and the direction you'd think his legs should be taking him, he's sort of slewing sideways as if he hit a patch of ice. It seems to go against the laws of physics—or at least the laws of locomotion as you understand them—and it leaves you shaking your head in bemused bafflement. How'd he do that?

Well, a puppy is a complex organism with a lot of parts, all of which don't necessarily grow at the same rate—including its legs. A difference of a fraction of an inch between one leg and the rest is huge,

resulting in a pup that naturally "lists" to one side or the other until everything "evens out." It's the same principle that makes a car with a flat tire want to turn to that side. If *both* legs on one side are shorter than the two on the other side, the effect is even more pronounced.

And if you believe that—I had you going, didn't I?—I have some oceanfront property in Nebraska that you might be interested in. Seriously, I think it's just part of the maturation process, something gangling puppies do until they develop the coordination and muscle control they need to get from point A to point B using as direct a route as possible—assuming they're not distracted along the way, which with puppies is always a distinct possibility.

Why do male puppies (and even some females) "mount" your leg?

You know what they say: practice makes perfect. The "mounting" behavior is completely normal among adolescent male dogs. It's nature way of making sure all the equipment's in good working order and preparing them for the real thing, analogous to the unbidden erections that plague boys at a comparable stage of sexual development. At that age they just happen, which is why you see so many boys in middle school walking hunched over with their hands jammed into their front pockets. (Or sitting at their desks after class pretending to write in their notebooks when in fact they're waiting for things to, um, subside, the way I used to when my busty seventh grade English teacher wore a tight-fitting sweater and I let my gaze linger a bit too long—like a nanosecond.)

And no, there's nothing special about legs; they're simply targets of opportunity, conveniently located and just the right size. Pillows, cushions, and stuffed animals are other common attention-getters, as are toddlers and even school-age kids crawling around on all fours. If the puppy belongs to you but the kid doesn't, these episodes can be pretty embarrassing.

Some females exhibit mounting behavior as well, typically those with a high level of testosterone and pronounced masculine tendencies—including male-like responses to bitches in season and rejection of males when they themselves are in estrus. If you want to call it homosexuality, be my guest. The good news is that this behavior usually runs its course well before the pup's first birthday; when it crops up in older dogs (and it does), the driving wheel is dominance, not sex.

Why are puppies so irresistible—and why do they always make us so happy?

I was going to talk about the 15,000 years (if not longer) that we've shared our homes and hearths with dogs, about the intricate workings of symbiosis and the mysteries of co-evolution, about how we've made the dog not in our own image but in the image of our idealized selves, the people we wish we were. I was going to talk about the way they know us better than we know ourselves, too, about their uncanny ability to tune into our emotional wavelength and give us what we need to get by. I was going to talk about our shared capacities for love and play, about loyalty and tolerance and faithfulness and all the other noble qualities the dog possesses, and I was going to make the argument that we have a kind of innate attraction to puppies, a bred-in-the-bone receptivity to everything they embody and represent.

But then I thought, 'Come on.' You might as well ask why the sun comes up, or why water is wet, or why the stars glitter in the night sky. If you want to know why puppies are irresistible, and why they make us happy, all you need to do is spend, oh, about two seconds in their swirling, squirming, frolicking company. There are realms words cannot illuminate, and the place puppies occupy in the human heart is one of them.